C000224588

# Forgiveness

## Series Preface

The volumes in NCP's "7 x 4" series offer a meditation a day for four weeks, a bite of food for thought, a reflection that lets a reader ponder the spiritual significance of each and every day. Small enough to slip into a purse or coat pocket, these books fit easily into everyday routines.

# Forgiveness

## Three Minute Reflections on Redeeming Life's Most Difficult Moments

### Joan Mueller

New City Press
Hyde Park, New York

Published in the United States by New City Press
202 Comforter Blvd., Hyde Park, NY 12538
www.newcitypress.com
©2012 Joan Mueller

Cover design by Durva Correia

Library of Congress Cataloging-in-Publication Data:

Mueller, Joan, 1956-
    Forgiveness : three minute reflections on redeeming life's most difficult
moments / Joan Mueller.
    p. cm.
    Includes bibliographical references.
    ISBN 978-1-56548-426-9 (pbk. : alk. paper) 1. Forgiveness--Religious
aspects--Christianity--Meditations. I. Title.
    BV4647.F55M84 2012
    242'.4--dc23

2011041378

Printed in the United States of America

# Contents

## one
### God Heals Our Wounds

## two
### Asking God to Forgive

# three
## Prayerfully Discerning God's Way

# four
## Love

# Introduction

Most human beings understand that forgiveness is essential to living a healthy and productive life. We know that the anger of resentment holds us back, ruins our health, and brings with it a dark outlook. As Christians, we want to give witness to others that our faith helps us get through tough times with grace and dignity.

Yet, there are moments when forgiveness becomes a challenge, and the very thought of forgiving someone who has hurt us seems to belittle our grief. A perpetrator might be unrepentant. In other instances, "things happen" in the background, in board rooms behind closed doors, and we don't even know who has hurt us. While we are left with devastating consequences, the rest of the world goes on as though nothing has happened.

There are wounds that permanently disfigure us, leaving us with a constant reminder of an injury. A drunk driver disables one for life. A sexual predator robs our self-confidence and self-esteem, and we struggle with post-traumatic stress disorder and depression while the perpetrator walks away. Someone hurts our child, and our anger becomes all-encompassing, eating us alive.

*Forgiveness* is written for two types of persons: those who are struggling with forgiveness, have significant wounds, and can't seem to find their way to healing; and Christians who are not dealing with a particular forgiveness issue, but are striving to make forgiveness a daily spiritual practice, because they know that forgiveness is essential to living a truly Christian life. For them, forgiveness becomes a spirituality that divinizes their way of living in the world.

Like other books in this series, *Forgiveness* features daily readings for a span of four weeks. Each day includes a scriptural passage, a short reflection, and a spiritual exercise. The first week deals with the need to recognize that God sees and desires to heal our wounds. The second follows Christ's example of asking God to forgive. The third addresses our temptation to seek vengeance and suggests how to prayerfully discern the way of God in the midst of our hurt. The fourth week invites us into loving service, even as we continue to be healed by the love of God and others.

Readers are encouraged to be gentle with themselves as they work through this book. Forgiveness is not easy and time is needed. Perhaps one will need to pray the exercises of one week for many weeks before moving forward. No problem. God asks us to forgive, and as long as we are "in process," we are moving toward God. As God is tender to us, so we also need to be tender with our own soul.

# God Heals
## Our Wounds

# Basking in God's Healing Love

I speak to encourage Jerusalem;
I will keep consoling her until she is healed
and her happiness shines like a torch
   in the night.
Jerusalem, the nations will see your salvation.
All their rulers will see your glory.
You will be called by a new name given
   to you especially by the Lord.

No longer will people consider you forsaken
   or your land deserted.
Rather, your new name shall mean,
   "God is pleased."
You will be God's crowning glory because
   God delights in you.

*Isaiah 62:1–5*

When we struggle with forgiveness we often feel alone in the world. We suffer with a hurt while the rest of the world seems to move forward without us. We go to work, raise our families, and take care of business while our hearts are breaking. If we pay attention to our pain, we feel we might break. If we deny it, we worry that the stress might do long-term harm.

There is a third option. God sees our pain and wishes to validate it. God notices our discouragement and wants to encourage us. God wants our happiness, not our suffering. God wants our glory, not our degradation.

## Spiritual Practice

Sometimes when we have been discouraged or downhearted we begin to believe that we somehow deserve our suffering. We begin to see ourselves as unloved and perhaps even unlovable. We begin to feel as though we are a bad person, a bad parent, or a bad spouse. God, however, despite whatever weakness we have or whatever we may have done, loves us, unconditionally.

During the day today, try to imagine God's radiant love shining on you. If this feels uncomfortable, just do the exercise for a couple of seconds, but try to repeat it at various times during the day. Be gentle with yourself. God has time, and the warmth of God's love promises healing.

# 2 Seeing with God's Eyes

Don't worry about the deeds of the wicked,
or be jealous of the success of those who do
wrong.
For they will soon whither like dried up grass;
and disappear like scorched plants.

Rather, trust in the Lord and keep doing good.
Seek your happiness in God and you will
    have what you desire.
Trust God and God will help you.
God will make you shine like the midday sun.

*Psalm 37:1–4*

When we are suffering, it sometimes seems that the rest of the world lives without suffering, that others are not suffering as we are. So often those who have hurt us move on with their lives, seemingly oblivious to the hurt they have caused us. We are just a blip on their screen, hardly worth their notice. Sometimes it seems as though the wicked win.

Scripture tells us that God judges the situation differently. God judges not our success, but the depth of our love and compassion. Our glory is how we reflect the love and compassion of God, not how we outshine our neighbor.

## Spiritual Practice

God doesn't see the world as we do. Heaven is the dream that love will be the voice that matters, that war will be no more, that children will always be treasured, and that the poor will have their voices heard. Heaven is an upside-down world, but it is a real world — it is the dwelling place of God.

Jesus did not promise us a life without suffering, but he did promise to heal us. This healing requires us to see as Jesus sees — to see from the perspective of heaven. This "seeing," because it is not our usual perspective, requires practice.

Today, try to look on your life and see it as Jesus views it. What does Jesus confirm about your life? Where does Jesus want to heal and console you? Allow God's compassionate eyes to rest upon you, little by little, until you become comfortable.

# 3 Crying Out to God

The Pharisees were complaining: "This man welcomes tax collectors and sinners." Hearing this, Jesus told them this parable:

A shepherd had a hundred sheep and lost one. What should he do? He leaves the ninety-nine together in the pasture and searches for the lost one until he finds it. When he finds it, he is so happy that he puts it on his shoulders and carries it back home. Then he calls his friends and neighbors together and says, "Rejoice with me, because I have found my lost sheep."

In just the same way, there will be more joy in heaven over one who repents than over ninety-nine respectable people who feel no need of repentance.

*Luke 15:1–7*

No matter who I am, God cares about me. If I feel insignificant, hurting, dirty, or sinful, God cares about me. If I feel lost, isolated, tangled in an impossible situation, God cares about me. If I feel shattered, invisible, wounded, God cares about me.

God cares about me and wishes to find me. Just as a lamb bleats when in trouble and in need of a shepherd, so we also are to cry out to God for help. God promises that we need only ask in order to receive. If we need consolation and peace, we need to ask for these gifts from God.

## Spiritual Practice

We know that God is searching for us, wants to find us. It's easier to find those who want to be found, who call out for help letting others know their willingness to be discovered. God's love and grace is available to us. God wants to care for us but waits upon our freedom. God is courteous and will not rush in if we do not want God's presence in our lives.

Try to identify what would make things better for you today. When doing this, stay within what is possible. It is not possible, for instance, to bring back someone who has died. But perhaps having people care for you during this time would be possible. Ask God to bring these people into your life. When we are hurting, we often wish that things were simply the way they used to be. When moving forward, we need to think of how God's grace might move us into the future. Try to identify what you need just for today and ask God for this grace.

# 4 Acting Out of Grace

There are different gifts, but the same Spirit. The Spirit gives one the gift of wisdom, and another the gift of knowledge. The Spirit blesses another with faith, and another with the power to heal. God's Spirit gives one person the power to speak God's message, while another has the gift of prayer. Yet, it is one and the same Spirit who blesses us with these gifts. We are blessed with God's grace as the Spirit wills.

*1 Corinthians 12:4–11*

Paul reminds us that every person is blessed by God, but that not all are blessed in the same way. The various circumstances and events of our lives become, if we permit this, blessings for both ourselves and for others. This doesn't mean that painful events do not remain painful, but that we have the potential to become wounded healers.

When God looks at your soul, what does God see? What gifts has God given you? The gift of compassion, tenderness, courage, self-confidence, or service? If your name was your grace, how would God call you?

## Spiritual Exercise

There is no healing without distinguishing what is sick from what is healthy. In prayer today, identify the grace in your own soul. What does God see within you apart from your wounds and hurt?

Try to name at least one gift of God that is within your soul and try to act out of this gift. If I have the gift of "baking," for example, I might make some cookies and bring them to work tomorrow. If I have the gift of "compassion," I might call a friend who is hurting and ask her out to lunch. If I have the gift of "communication," I might text or e-mail a friend or two just to let them know I'm thinking about them. Try to act out of grace today rather than out of hurt.

# 5 Pondering God's "Case" for Us

The Lord says,
"When Israel was a child, I loved him.
It was I who taught him to walk.
I took my people in my arms, but they did
    not acknowledge my care for them.
I caressed them with tenderness and love;
    picking them up, I held them to my cheek.
I bent down and fed them.

Yet, they refuse to come to me;
they insist on turning away.

How can I give you up, Israel?
How could I ever abandon you?
It is impossible for my heart to do this,
    for I love you too much!
My anger cannot overpower my love,
    for I am God!
I, the Holy One, will remain with you."

*Hosea 1:3–9*

When difficult things happen in life, sometimes our very faith is shaken. "Where is God in all of this?" Our trust is weakened.

Forgiveness is the love of God that persists even during our most difficult days. Cut off from God, we cannot forgive. Only God's love can pierce through righteous anger. God's love is beyond anger, and persistently reaches out to us no matter what the offense.

## Spiritual Exercise

Reflect today on the worst thing that you have ever done. Did other people forgive you this offense? Did God forgive you?

Now, imagine another who has hurt or is hurting you. Is there anything that God wants you to do to keep yourself safe and healthy in this situation? Are you willing to do this? How does God perceive the perpetrator? How does God perceive you?

# 6 Sharing our Sorrow with Jesus

If you find yourself burdened, come to me,
and I will give you rest.
Take up my yoke and learn from me,
for I am gentle and humble of heart
and you will find rest for your soul.
For my yoke is easy,
and my burden is light.

*Matthew 11:28–30*

Emotional wounds burden us. When we are faced with the betrayal of friends, lovers, or peers, we feel isolated. When we are challenged with irreparable consequences at the hands of another, we find ourselves angry and full of anxiety. When others hurt us and walk away as though nothing has happened, we feel worthless and invisible.

In the midst of this, Jesus understands and sees our burden. Jesus was betrayed, alone, isolated, and judged worthless. If misery loves company, Jesus, at least, is an understanding companion.

## Spiritual Exercise

We Christians have a God who has shared our sorrow. Today, whenever you feel overwhelmed with sorrow, hurt, or anger, try to picture Jesus at your side. When you look at Jesus, recall the sorrow, hurt, and anger that he must have felt when abandoned by his friends, betrayed by his companions, or left to die by members of his beloved religion. Try to sympathize with Jesus in his sorrow, even as you allow Jesus to sympathize with the sorrow of your life.

# 7 Appreciating the Light of God's Glory

We hold God's glory within us in clay pots to show that this glory is God's not ours. We may be troubled, but never defeated. We sometimes suffer doubt, but never despair. We have enemies, but always have a friend. We can be badly hurt, but we are not crushed.

*2 Corinthians 4:7–9*

God became human so that we could become adopted sons and daughters of God. We are adopted within the Trinitarian family of God. The light in our eyes reveals the wonder of our souls, the spark of our life, the very glory of God. Although we suffer sickness, doubt, and betrayal, this glory of God revealed in the very light in our eyes still shines through our weakness. God does not abandon us, even if we are tempted to abandon ourselves.

## Spiritual Exercise

Every time you look into a mirror today, study for a minute the light of God's glory within your eyes. Peer into this light and spend a moment thanking God for the beauty of your soul. Affirm this beauty, even if you feel tired or doubtful of your own worth. Remember, you are giving God glory by praising the glory of your soul that God has created.

We know that God does not create junk, and certainly God's glory within you needs to be treasured. Try to praise God today for the treasure of your life, for the treasure of your soul. Try also to make an effort to see the same light of God's glory in the eyes of those you meet today. How might this vision change your way of relating to them?

# Asking God to Forgive

# two

# Inviting God's Forgiveness

Some men carrying a paralyzed man tried to bring him into the house where Jesus was teaching. Because the crowd was large, they could not find a way to bring him in, so they carried him up to the roof, made an opening in the tiles, and lowered his litter into the crowd in front of Jesus. Jesus, admiring their faith, said to the man, "My friend, your sins are forgiven."

The Pharisees and teachers of the law murmured to themselves, "Who is this man who speaks such blasphemy? Only God is able to forgive sins!"

*Luke 5:17–21*

As Christians, sometimes we forget that Jesus was a good Jew. He knew the Jewish law, spent time with those who studied it, and followed the spirit of the Torah wholeheartedly. He knew that only God could forgive sins, and he was not looking to pick a fight with the Jewish leaders. He did not say to the paralyzed man, "I forgive your sins" but rather put the phrase in the passive voice, "Your sins *are forgiven*."

Jesus proclaimed not his own power to forgive, but the power of God's forgiveness. This is wonderful for those of us who wish to follow Jesus. Even if we feel helpless to forgive, we can trust the power of God to forgive.

## Spiritual Exercise

Imagine today an issue where you find forgiveness challenging. Try to honor your feelings around this situation. Do you find it difficult to forgive? Are you still angry about the situation? Do you still feel hurt?

If so, do not worry. It is not up to you to forgive, since, as Jesus knew so well, "only God can forgive." With this in mind, imagine the one(s) who have hurt you and speak the words of Jesus, "Your sins are forgiven." As you do this, remember that it is the power of God, not your power or feelings, that is able to forgive. If you feel the need to be forgiven yourself, use the same words and trust that God has the power to forgive you.

# 2 Asking for God's Blessings

Listen, Lord, and answer me for I am
  helpless and weak.
Save me from death, for I am faithful to you.
Save me, your servant, who trusts in you.

Be merciful to me, for you are my God.
To you I pray all day long.
Bless me, Lord, for my prayers rise to you.
You are good and forgiving,
full of faithful love to those who pray to you.

*Psalm 86:1–5*

When we suffer from evil, we often want nothing more but the chance to return to our former happiness. When we are on our knees, we count on God to be faithful to us, and hope that somehow God will come through for us.

When we suffer, we need God to show us mercy. We need God to heal our sorrow, to comfort us. In our sorrow, we sometimes come face to face with our raw emotions, our own potential to hurt others, and perhaps even our own sin. On our knees before God we ask for everything at once — mercy, healing, forgiveness, and blessing.

## Spiritual Exercise

Which of the gifts mentioned by the psalmist — mercy, healing, forgiveness, blessing — do you need the most? Do you need one, two, all four of these gifts? Spend time today listening to the wounds of your heart. Gently ask God for what you need, knowing that God, in God's mercy, will hear your prayer.

# 3 Pondering God's Forgiveness

> They refused to obey you, they forgot all you
>   did.
> In their pride they chose a leader
>   who returned them to slavery in Egypt.
> But you are a forgiving God,
>   gracious and loving, slow to anger.
> Your mercy is great, you did not forsake them.
>
> *Nehemiah 9:17*

Sometimes human beings do bad things. They disobey God. They make bad decisions, and at times, these decisions affect the lives of the innocent. Nehemiah mentions those who made bad choices and were sold into slavery as a consequence. They had children who were innocent, and their actions affected populations that were innocent. Sometimes we are caught in the dragnet of other people's sins. Sometimes, we must admit, others are caught in the dragnet of our sins.

While we sin, God is always faithful. God forgives and heals. God is slow to anger and does not forsake us.

## Spiritual Exercise

Imagine for a moment that you have died, gone to heaven, and are invited to your first great heavenly banquet. You are dressed in a beautiful white robe and led by an angel into the banquet hall. When you look at the long rows of tables, you notice that there are name tags at the places.

Listen to your heart. Is there anyone with whom you would not wish to be seated? Is there anyone who might refuse to sit next to you?

Be gentle with yourself in this. If you really can't sit next to someone, ask, in your imagination, your guiding angel to beg God to heal your anger and hurt. There is no time in heaven, so hanging around in the reception area for a while longer is no problem. Take your time and, if necessary, negotiate a more comfortable seating arrangement with your angel.

# 4 Praising God in the Midst of Our Pain

Remember this, Israel, my servant.
I have created you and will never forget you.
I have swept your sins away like a cloud,
your sins are forgotten like the morning mist.
Come back to me for I am the one
    who saves you.

Shout for joy, you heavens!
Earth, mountains and every tree in the forest
    break into song!
For the Lord has shown his greatness
    by saving his people Israel.

*Isaiah 44:21–23*

A highly publicized media trial once featured a victim's family who continued to fight their legal battle against a murderer. Even with all the publicity in the world, this family expressed the isolation and frustration they felt. Their lives had been torn apart by a perpetrator who had invaded their family and personal lives. Even as the perpetrator sat in prison, he remained aloof and seemingly unaffected, while the victims' lives continued to be torn apart.

When we are hurt, we sometimes feel forgotten. When we suffer an action that permanently changes our lives, we wish we could wake up from what seems like a bad dream. In Isaiah, God says that our sins will be swept away like a cloud or forgotten like the morning mist. Both clouds and mist do change the face of the earth, but they pass and we forget them eventually. Can one hope that life after a significant hurt could truly be healed?

## Spiritual Exercise

God asks Israel to trust that God can bring healing and, in the meanwhile, to join nature in its song of praise to God. We are to shout the praise of God and sing, even as we hold sorrow in our hearts.

Try to identify today a mantra or a song of praise to God. Do not push to try to make everything better. Simply do as God asks, and praise God even in the midst of your suffering. Look for the beauty of life today and praise God for this beauty.

# 5 Praying for Reparation

I write to you, my children,
  so that you do not sin.
But if anyone does sin, we have someone
  who pleads with the Father on our behalf,
Jesus Christ, the righteous one.
For Christ himself is the means by which
  our sins are forgiven.
And not only our sins, but the sins of all.

*John 2:1–2*

Even though most of us do not commit heinous crimes, all of us sin. Sometimes we fail to respect ourselves. We fail to appreciate the beauty of our soul, we compromise our health with foolish eating habits or unnecessary stress. We play God by depriving ourselves of sleep or other necessities.

At other times, we fail to appreciate the souls of others. We snub some and criticize others. We see others merely as means to our end, without considering the hurtfulness of our disregard. We use others for our own emotional, physical, or spiritual needs without reflecting how this might affect the other.

## Spiritual Exercise

I once lived with a Franciscan sister who understood how little — sometimes even thoughtless — actions had the potential to be hurtful to others. Every night she prayed, "Jesus, Repairer, repair for me." This prayer summarizes what John is saying. It is Jesus who pleads with God for our forgiveness. It is through Jesus that we are forgiven.

Today, try to pray, "Jesus, Repairer, repair for me" while you are driving, exercising, doing dishes, etc. If this is comfortable, next try to pray for the one(s) who have hurt you, for example, "Jesus, Repairer, repair for Bob." Again, be gentle with yourself and pray as you are able.

# 6 Imagining the Family of God

Out of love, God decided to adopt us
  as God's children through Jesus Christ.
This was God's will and delight.
Let us praise God for this wondrous gift,
for this grace he bestowed on us
  in his beloved Son.
For, through the blood of Christ we have
  been set free — our sins are forgiven.
How great is this grace that God has given us!

*Ephesians 1:5–8*

Christians say they are "saved," but what does this mean? In his letter to the Ephesians, Paul outlines one meaning. Christ came to earth and, despite our sins and unworthiness, chose to adopt us as sons and daughters into the very family of God. We know that God is love — the love between the Father, Son, and Holy Spirit. Through Jesus Christ we participate in the love dynamics of the family of God.

In a family, love demands much of us. We sacrifice for our children, we endure petty comments, we work long hours, all because we love our children and spouse. In return, these sacrifices promote our family life — promote the love upon which the very concept of family depends.

## Spiritual Exercise

Although we know that we are not God, as Christians we believe that we are adopted sons and daughters of God through Jesus Christ. Because of this adoption, we belong to the family of God — a family characterized by love.

Belonging to this family means that Christians hope to share all eternity in loving union with the Father, Son, Holy Spirit, and their neighbors. In the family of God, love of God is also love of neighbor, since all are joined in the loving union who is God. Today, try to imagine yourself in this family of God. Speak with the Father, Jesus, and the Holy Spirit about your struggles to love and forgive. Ask for any grace you might need in your life to help you love and forgive your neighbor.

# 7 Reviewing our Relationships

Happy are those whose sins are forgiven,
whose wrongs are pardoned.
Happy are those whom the Lord
   does not accuse of wrongdoing,
whose hearts hold no lie.

When I did not confess my sins,
I wore myself out day and night
   with anguish.

The wicked will suffer sorrow,
but those who trust in the Lord are protected
   by God's constant love.
Be glad and rejoice, you who are righteous!
Sing for joy all you who are upright of heart!

*Psalm 32:1–3; 8*

We know that when we are guilty of some offense, we are not at peace. We know that when we have hurt someone who we love, we feel miserable. We know that when others have betrayed our trust or abused our good will, our relationship with them is strained.

God's forgiveness brings peace. What God asks is that we speak with God about any breaks of love within the Trinitarian family. If I am at odds with my neighbor, I need to let God know about this. Otherwise, I toss and turn alone, wearing myself out day and night, as the psalmist says.

## Spiritual Exercise

Today, examine closely your relationships. Who is closest to you? Do they know how much they mean to you? What relationships do you find challenging in your life? Are there relationships that are broken? Do you harbor hatred for anyone?

Without judging yourself or others, simply tell God today about the status of your relationships. Perhaps today might be a day to send a beloved person in your life flowers or a message of care and concern. If there is someone with whom you are not at peace, hold this broken relationship up to God whenever they enter your consciousness and ask that God heal this injury.

# Prayerfully Discerning
## God's Way

three

# 1 Walking with God and Others

When I come to worship, what shall I bring
   the Lord of heaven?
Shall I offer God the best calves to burn
   as an offering?
Might God be pleased with thousands
   of sheep or endless streams of olive oil?
Should I sacrifice my first-born child
   as atonement for my sins?

No, the Lord has told you what is good
   and what is required:
Do what is just, be faithful in love,
   and walk humbly as a companion of God.

*Micah 6:6–8*

What does God desire for me? What is God's will for my life? Micah sums it up beautifully. God doesn't want me to sacrifice my health. God does not want to hurt me, my family, or my friends. God is not vindictive.

Rather, we are to worship God and serve our neighbor. If we are all living as adopted children in the family of God, then it is our duty and dignity to love our neighbor. Yet, given that others cannot always be trusted, how is it possible to love all people? We know how to love family and friends, but how are we to act in the world?

Micah explains succinctly. We are to do what is just — do the right thing. We are to be constant in love — faithful in our care of others. We are to walk humbly as God's companion — imagine ourselves not alone but in loving relationship with God and others.

## Spiritual Exercise

Spend a few minutes examining your life today according to Micah's instructions. In your family, friendships, and work life are you doing the right thing? Are there places where you cheat a bit, are stingy, or disruptive? Are you faithful in your care of others? Do you know a vulnerable person who needs compassion? Do you faithfully take care of your own soul? Do you remember to walk through life with God as a companion, or do you walk alone?

# 2 Seeing from God's Perspective

I offer my prayer to you, O Lord,
in you I trust.
Save me from the shame of defeat,
and do not let my enemies gloat over me.

Teach me your ways, O Lord,
make them known to me.
Teach me how to live according to your truth
for you are the God who saves me.
I trust always in you.

Remember, O Lord, your kindness
    and faithful love
that you have revealed long ago.
Forgive my sins and remember me, Lord,
    in your constant love.
The Lord is righteous and good,
God shows sinners the path they
    must follow.
The Lord leads the humble on the path
    of righteousness
and teaches them God's will.

*Psalm 25:1–5*

The psalmist prays to God but feels defeated. Asking for help, the psalmist begs to be taught and blessed with the kindness and faithful love of God. Trusting in God even in the midst of defeat, the psalmist knows that God is good and trustworthy. When we are down, we need to allow God to teach us how to see from God's perspective.

## Spiritual Exercise

When life throws us a curve ball, we often find ourselves out of balance. Our faith can be challenged, our peace compromised, and our perspective short-sighted.

In life, when we lack skills, we often seek education in order to open up new opportunities. We need to do the same in our spiritual life. The psalmist indicates that the teacher we need is God. Only God can teach us how to see from God's perspective.

To move forward, we must leave the vision of the past behind and trust that God has a vision for our future. Even if evil has interfered with our life, God is endlessly creative and can dream a future for us. Today, gently ask God to teach you to see from God's perspective and try to open yourself to the possibility of a new future.

# 3 Noticing Our Conversations

God chooses those whom the world considers nobodies in order to shame those "in the
know." God chooses the weak, in order to
confound the powerful. God chooses those
whom the world snubs in order to bring
down the self-important. No one is to boast
in God's presence.

God has brought us into union with Christ
Jesus, and has given us Christ as our wisdom. Through Christ, we are brought into
union with God. Through Christ, we are set
free and become holy. Therefore, as scripture says, "Let anyone who boasts, boast of
what God has done!"

*1 Corinthians 1:27–31*

When we are overlooked, snubbed, or con-
sidered outsiders, we have, perhaps, a better
chance of understanding that all true wisdom
and grace comes from God rather than from
ourselves. If we are not pursuing power or
riches, we have the time and emotional energy
to dedicate ourselves to the love and care of

others. We have the tenderness to treasure a small bird near our window or to see the fragile hand of a child.

What do I brag about when I am with friends? What is the topic of my conversation? Am I an "I-centered" person always boasting about my achievements and personal gains? Does my conversation reflect healthy relationships with family and friends? Do I ever talk about the beauty and wonder of life, of creation, of God's work?

## Spiritual Exercise

As you go about the day today, notice the topics of your conversations. What do you speak about? What do your friends and coworkers speak about? If your conversation seems "I-centered," try to refocus the next conversation on the treasured relationships of your life. If you find that you lack a certain sense of wonder and praise in your conversation, try to notice and appreciate the wonder of creation in a flower, tree, or animal. Praise God for this wonder.

As you notice your conversations today, are there any trends that you would like to change? If so, what might you do to become more positive, more relational, or more filled with God's praise?

# 4 Asking for God's Compassionate Healing

A leper came to Jesus, knelt before him, and begged him: "If you want to, you can make me well." Jesus had compassion on him, and reaching out to touch him said: "Of course, I want to, be healed!"

*Mark 1:40*

When we would like to make changes in our lives, we sometimes find that we are less in command of our moral aptitude than we would like. We think that we can will ourselves into goodness and grace, but in reality we find that our resolutions fall flat.

The leper in today's reading was wise. He knew that he could not cure himself, so he reached out to Jesus for help. Similarly, we cannot cure ourselves of many things. We need the help and compassionate grace of God. To receive it, all we need to do is ask for it. God will not disregard our free will, our freedom. If we want a tender and compassionate relationship with God, we need to ask for what we need, so that God might say to us, "Of course, I want to, be healed."

## Spiritual Exercise

Spend a few minutes before God today discerning what in your life is in need of healing. Is there a relationship that is painfully broken? Do you have a bad habit or addiction that you are unable to break? Is your job a challenging ordeal rather than a source of fruitful labor? What situation or condition makes you feel helpless?

Imagine now reaching out to God with this issue in your hands. Ask, gently, that God heal this wound, knowing that God is compassionate and merciful. Trust in God's wisdom and tenderness and put aside any notion that God might punish you. Listen, instead, to the words of Jesus, "Of course, I want to, be healed!"

# 5 Discerning our Company

Surely he bore our grief and suffered our sorrows. But we judged him to be punished and afflicted by God. Yet he was wounded for our faults and beaten for our iniquities. We are healed because of the sufferings he bore, made whole by the wounds he received. We were all like lost sheep, every one astray and alone. But the Lord laid upon him the sins of us all.

*Isaiah 53:4–5*

If the Lord were present among us, would we see him? Do we notice those who seem afflicted and sorrowful? Do we only hang around the successful and financially blessed? Are there people in our lives we ignore?

Sometimes those who appear judged and afflicted by God are, in reality, blessed. Spending time with them can bring us real and godly blessings. While our social circle might provide us with a certain normalcy, being outside the group can inspire freedom and creativity. Isaiah suggests that God is often found on the outside.

## Spiritual Exercise

Spend time pondering today the people in your life who you have judged to be outsiders. Revisit these judgments and try to discern why you made them. Are you fearful of these people? Do you worry that they might be emotional or financial "black holes"? Are you afraid that they might be violent?

Now consider those with whom you choose to associate. Do they offer you creativity and freedom, or mere conformity? Are you fearful of them? Do they drain you emotionally or financially? Are they violent in any way?

We want to keep company that inspires us, frees us, and encourages us to be faithful to our relational commitments. If our company is violent, things must change immediately. If our company is merely conformist and uncreative, we need to make some new friends. Contrary to our instincts, the people that can bring us the most life and freedom can, at times, be found on the fringes.

# 6 Enjoying the Gift of Praise

Praise the Lord, my soul!
Let all my being praise God's holy name!
Praise the Lord my soul!
Do not forget God's kindness!

God forgives my sins
and heals my sickness!
God saves me from death
and blesses me with love and mercy!

God fills my life with blessings
and heals all your sicknesses.

*Psalm 103:1–4*

Today's reading is delightful, asking us simply to praise God. Why should we sing God's praise? Because God has given us many blessings. In the midst of the challenges of life, we are to remember that God has been kind to us. God has given us personal gifts, wonderful relationships, the beauty of nature, and perhaps even a bit of luck now and then.

Most likely, we have made a few mistakes and God has willingly overlooked these. We have moved on without much consequence. We have been blessed.

## Spiritual Exercise

Today, spend a few minutes thinking about the blessings that have been a part of your life. What in your childhood, teenage years, adult years was truly blessed? What are your personal gifts and blessings? What relationships have brought you true blessings?

As you recall these blessings, thank God for them one-by-one, or hold them all together in your mind and sing a song of praise to God. If sorrow or preoccupation enter your mind, gently set these concerns aside and enjoy the simple praise of God.

# 7 Surrendering our Sorrow into God's Hands

About noon, the sun stopped shining. Darkness covered the entire region until about
three o'clock, and the curtain of the Temple
was torn in two. Jesus cried out in a loud
voice: "Father, into your hands I commend
my spirit!" After he said this, he died.

*Luke 23:44–45*

Luke's Gospel has a unique, challenging, and
spiritually rich theology of forgiveness. On the
cross, Jesus prays: "Father, forgive them" — not
"I forgive you"! — "they don't know what they
do." Jesus, in his moment of grave sorrow and
pain, does not rely on his own power to forgive,
but rather calls out to his Father. For Luke, asking
God to forgive is what forgiveness means.

Once we ask God to forgive those who hurt
us, what do we do with our pain and the hurtful
consequences of what has been done to us?
Luke helps us again with this dilemma in the
above reading. On the cross, instead of using
his last breath to curse his murderers, Jesus

surrenders his spirit into the hands of God. Even with his last breath, Jesus chooses love — not an easy choice.

## Spiritual Exercise

As you take your walk or travel by car to the office, the store, or wherever life takes you today, try to keep the two forgiveness prayers of Jesus in your heart. Think gently of those who have hurt you and ask God to forgive them — "Father, forgive them, they do not know what they do." When you find that you have left-over hurt and pain, place this in God's hands and ask for healing — "Father, into your hands I commend my spirit." Trust God with your sorrow, knowing that God promises you healing.

Love

four

# Choosing Love as Our Identity

Beloved, let us love one another,
because love is from God;
everyone who loves is born of God
and knows God.

*1 John 4:7–8*

Love and grace are God's gift to us, but God does not force them upon us. Rather God waits for us to choose the way of grace. Love is also our mission. God asks that we let go of cheap judgments in order to embrace the unique presence of God among us who is our neighbor. We are God's hands, feet, and heart in the world.

Even if others have let me down, if I can no longer trust as innocently as I used to, God's love wants me, wounded as I am, as an instrument of love in the world. Those who pursue truth without love are deceived, for love is from God and distinguishes those who know God.

## Spiritual Exercise

Today, do all you can to choose the way of love in your life. When you are tempted to be short with someone, step back and choose to be graceful. If you have the habit of excluding someone from your circle, take the initiative and actively include the person today.

Some find it difficult to love those outside of their immediate family and friends. It is challenging to trust those we do not know. Others find it harder to appreciate those close to them. While they wear themselves out in the care of strangers, they are short-tempered with those at home. Today, identify where you feel "love-challenged," and do what you can to love those you find more difficult. While God may not ask us to change the world, we are identified as Christians by the love that we have for others. Choose today to make love your identity in the world.

# 2 Shining God's Love on All

But I say to you: Love your enemies and pray
for those who persecute you, so that you
   may be
children of your Father in heaven;
   for he makes
his sun rise on the evil and on the good,
   and sends
rain on the righteous and on the unrighteous.

*Matthew 5:44–45*

What if God were more like us? What if rain fell only on the fields of the worthy, if children were blessed strictly on the merits of their parents, if God allowed the sun to shine only on those who merited God's favor. Obviously, this would be a different world, perhaps a world in which we all fervently courted God's favor, not for love, but to obtain rewards.

Of course, God does not want our obedience in return for rewards; God wants our true love. As a father who cherishes his children, God does not count our righteous actions or dole out punishments according to our merits. Rather,

God chooses the way of love. The sun shines on all; the rain refreshes all.

## Spiritual Exercise

Every family, every person experiences those who reek havoc on their peace. Sometimes our greatest challenge comes from within our family; other times, from our workplace, church, or social network. Try to identify today anyone who might challenge your peace and pray for them.

There are times, especially if the other is abusive, when prayer is all we can do. If we reach out in loving action to this person, we might be further hurt. Today, if it is possible to be tender towards the brother or sister who challenges us, do this. If not, actively love someone else in honor of the one who challenges you. Love freely and without strings, since God's love shines on all.

God calls us to be brothers and sisters in the family of God. Forming the bonds of family requires work, sacrifice, and unconditional love. Being the family of God also demands our effort and resources. Today, celebrate your presence in the family of God and do all you can to let God's love within you shine upon all.

# 3 Taking the First Step to Love

Do not judge your neighbor.
When the Lord comes,
he will bring to light what is hidden
   in darkness
and will manifest the motives of our hearts.
At that time, all will receive their praise
   from God.

*1 Corinthians 4:5*

We know how hurtful it is to be judged or maligned by others. Yet, most of us must admit that we, too, are guilty of judging others, of reducing their souls to disparaging caricatures. When we do this, we denigrate the creative genius of God expressed in unique ways through individual souls. Other people are not us. They think differently, act differently, even respond to God's voice in different ways. These differences express the creativity of God.

God creates us in God's image. A judgmental spirit accuses God of making a mistake. God, we think, should have made all people in our own image. We, rather than God, become the standard by which we judge others. We demean the grandeur of God's creativity, and demand to judge others by our own standard.

We are gifts to each other precisely because we are unique. We experience love in the sharing of our gifts of personality, talents, and treasure with each other. Instead of judging each other, we are to look for every opportunity to love.

## Spiritual Exercise

Trusting that God will take care to make things right in the end, continue today to focus on loving unconditionally. Wake up this morning and focus your attention on the opportunities you have to love. Since God's grace has been freely given to us, be enthusiastically altruistic with this grace, knowing that God will replenish those who respond to being God's hands, feet, and heart in the world.

Jesus did not focus on changing the world but on loving the neighbor before him. Do the same. Our lives are basically all local, and our circles are limited. Certainly it cannot be hard to reach out to those we meet today with a kind word, a tender gesture, or a gentle prayer. As God has given freely and enthusiastically, so freely and enthusiastically give. Focus your attention not on selfish preoccupation but on the creative mission of loving your neighbor.

# 4 Bringing Love's Balance to the World

Love your neighbor as yourself.

*Matthew 19:19*

In the *Spiritual Exercises*, St. Ignatius employs the principle of *agere contra*, Latin for "to move against." An individual soul must identify its propensity and move contrary to this natural inclination in order to bring balance. If, for instance, I have a tendency to love myself, to take care of my needs, and to think about my own good, then, to move toward balance, I must refocus my attention on loving others, taking care of the needs of others, and thinking about their good.

Others, however, may have a different propensity. They wear themselves out caring for others' needs. If they fail to take time to love themselves, they will soon become burned out, frustrated, and angry. We cannot give others fuel if there is nothing in our tank!

## Spiritual Exercise

Ask yourself today, do I love myself? Do I give myself the time I need to rest and heal? Is my self-talk positive? Do I engage in recreation and enjoy the friendship of others? Am I gentle with myself?

Then, ask yourself, do I love others? Do I take the time to listen to others and enjoy their company? When I speak about others do I give them the benefit of the doubt? Do I find that I have many friends who are radically different from me, or are those in my inner circle basically clones? Do others experience me to be a tender person?

Using Ignatius's principle of *agere contra*, balance your life today by focusing on what seems a bit unnatural to you. If you tend to care for yourself, focus today on your neighbor. Take every opportunity to be interested in others, and to attend to their needs. If you tend to place the needs of others above your own, spend time today tending to your own needs, remembering that if we do not love ourselves, we cannot truly love our neighbor.

# 5 Stretching My Heart for Love

> I am free, not a slave, but I make myself a slave in order to win over as many people as possible. When I am with those who are weak in faith, I become weak in order to gain them. I become all things to all for the sake of the gospel.
>
> *1 Corinthians 9:19, 22–23.*

When we are in the company of others, it is usually clear if people are really interested in us, listening to us, and understanding our perspective. If they interrupt us, or interpret our words only according to their own vision of reality, we might feel as though we are selling our treasures to those who have no appreciation for them. To understand the other, we must truly see life from their perspective.

A full, rich life is a life that engages with many people, many ideas, and many challenges. Those in a different socio-economic bracket than I will see life in radically different ways. Those from foreign cultures understand even the basics such as family, loyalty, and friendship differently. Understanding life from their perspective requires careful and humble listening. This act of stretching my vision will ultimately enrich my life and enlarge my heart.

## Spiritual Exercise

As you go about your day, reflect on the person or persons whom you find puzzling. Do you wonder why illegal immigrants risk life, limb, and family to cross borders? Do you puzzle about how an ethnic group in your community understands basic values? Do you shake your head over the attitudes of the young?

Today, purposefully try to understand life from the perspective of those who puzzle you. Listen to a young person without judgment or corrective comment. Search the Internet for stories about those whose presence you find problematic. Purposefully spend time with some who are not in your ordinary social circle and listen to their story, their perspective.

# 6 Sharing God's Love in the World

I was hungry and you fed me,
  naked and you clothed me.
I was sick and you nursed me,
  imprisoned and you visited me.
For as often as you did these things
  for one of the least,
    you did it for me!

*Matthew 25:35–36; 40*

Often, while we are generous in donating to the hungry, naked, and imprisoned, our lives are sheltered from them. We keep those with problems segregated in a certain part of town, lock criminals up, or avoid the hospital for fear of contagion. The gospel, however, asks us for more.

Jesus tells us that people know we are sons and daughters of God by the quality of our love for those who are unlike us. This sort of love is an active love that purposefully seeks out those who we would not associate with normally. God's presence tabernacles within each of our souls. Seeking out that presence in every soul is our mission. We hunger for souls because we hunger for God's presence, which we find in our neighbor, especially those whom the world considers to be "the least."

## Spiritual Exercise

Who is hungry, naked, sick, or imprisoned in your life? What are your connections to them? Have you avoided them? Have you found it difficult to make time in your life for them?

Today, take the first step to change this. Choose one — hungry, naked, sick, or imprisoned. When you have made your choice, determine how you will share your treasures with those less fortunate, knowing that this effort is the path to God. It is not so difficult to find God's presence within our circle, but when we seek the glory of God in the souls of those different than we are, we find the fullness of God.

# 7 Finding God's Presence in Our Midst

I say to you, if two of you agree on earth
about what to pray for, it will be done for you
by my Father in heaven.
For where two or three are gathered
   in my name,
there I am in their midst.

*Matthew 18:20*

When we listen together to the words of scripture, the Lord challenges us to love each other unconditionally. While we might think that loving each other within the context of prayer or of liturgy is easy, we know from our experience of church that it is not. Perhaps there is no wound as painful as the wounds we receive from our prayer companions. We expect to be safe when we gather for prayer, but we know that even our prayer gatherings can present challenges.

During Matthew's time, it was extremely difficult to gather for prayer. Some Jews thought that Jesus was the Messiah. Others felt that another Messiah would come. The Romans had all but destroyed the Temple, and the Jews were left with the question of how to live their faith in a world that no longer had its priests or Temple sacrifices. In this context, Matthew has Jesus give his followers clear instructions. When they gathered together, they were to agree in prayer. If they would work together, if they would love one another, they would discover him in their midst.

## Spiritual Exercise

Today as you live and work among your family and friends, try to be a grace-bearer in your world. Listen to the needs of others, to the hearts of others, and try to respond with tenderness and compassion. As you say "yes" to this grace of God, pay attention to those who are more experienced on this same path. Appreciate the grace of others, even as you attempt to be constantly open to the grace of God in your own life.

Whenever you have an experience of God, an experience of unity within your faith community, know that God is in your midst. Work to promote this unity and peace especially when you gather in prayer with others. When we are united in love, service, and worship, we share in the bonds of the Trinitarian family — we are true sons and daughters of God!

Also available in the same series:

**Praying Advent**
Three Minute Reflections on Peace, Faithfulness,
Joy, and Light
*Joan Mueller*
ISBN: 978-1-56548-358-3

**Keepsakes for the Journey**
Four Weeks on Faith Deepening
*Susan Muto*
ISBN: 978-1-56548-333-0

**Pathways to Relationship**
Four Weeks on Simplicity, Gentleness, Humility, Friendship
*Robert F. Morneau*
ISBN: 978-1-56548-317-0

**Pathways to Community**
Four Weeks on Prudence, Justice, Fortitude and Temperance
*Robert F. Morneau*
ISBN: 978-1-56548-303-3

**Pathways to God**
Four Weeks on Faith, Hope and Charity
*Robert F. Morneau*
ISBN: 978-1-56548-286-9

**Peace of Heart**
Reflections on Choices in Daily Life
*Marc Foley*
ISBN: 978-1-56548-293-7

To order call 1-800-462-5980
or e-mail orders@newcitypress.com